Poetry Decides
Kumar Mukul

कविता तय करती है
Translated by- Shivam Tomar

प्रभाकर प्रकाशन

ISBN: 978-93-56825-04-8
eISBN: 978-93-56825-61-1

© लेखकाधीन

प्रकाशक: प्रभाकर प्रकाशन
प्लॉट नं.-55, मेन मदर डेयरी रोड
पांडव नगर, ईस्ट दिल्ली-110092
फोन: 011-40395855

ई-मेल: sales@pharosbooks.in
वेबसाइट: www.prabhakarprakashan.com

आवरण चित्र: सैफ अंसारी

प्रथम संस्करण: 2024

मुद्रक: सुषमा बुक बाइंडिंग हाउस ओखला इंडस्ट्रियल
एरिया फेस-II, नई दिल्ली-110020

Poetry Decides (कविता तय करती है)
Kumar Mukul

Translated by - Shivam Tomar

Contents

Forward

The Illuminated Corners of Human Experience: The Poetry of Kumar Mukul

In Kumar Mukul's poetry collection, readers are taken on a profound journey through the labyrinth of human emotions and existential queries. Each poem is a universe unto itself, exploring the nuances of love, the allure of nature, the complexities of social norms, and the darker facets of human conduct.

With a language both accessible and deeply layered, he asks us to ponder what it truly means to be alive, to love, and to coexist. He is a master weaver of thoughts, emotions, ethereal concepts, and profound paradoxes, with linguistic finesse and lyrical beauty.

In his poem "The Best Letters," he unveils the ineffable magic of correspondence, "They may have fuzzy words but can still reflect a face." The poem serves as an allegory for understanding—the letters we never get, the words we never say, yet somehow know, in the depths of our being, exist.

In "Mountains," Kumar Mukul portrays nature as a sentient, almost spiritual entity, questioning why "clouds are dashing toward the mountains despite knowing that they will perish the moment they meet them." The symbiosis of nature and man becomes a metaphor for human desires and limitations, illuminating the intricate dynamics of belonging and longing.

His treatise on love in "Van Gogh's Ursula" is both haunting and uplifting. Through the prism of historical figures, he discusses love as an "ailment of the soul," exploring the dichotomies and harmonies that it ignites. "In their determination to save Ursula, they kill the Ursula within themselves," he writes, encapsulating love's complex intricacies with heartbreaking lucidity.

With poems like "September 11," Kumar Mukul doesn't shy away from scrutinizing the darker facets of human nature. He strips away pretense to confront the cyclical violence that humanity inflicts upon itself. In "Moon, On a Tough Day" and "Tragedies," he portrays the role of externalities in human perception—why we find "one's pain so enticing" and how the moon can serve as a solace or reminder of our isolation.

"I am a Hindu" is a poignant exploration of identity that starkly captures the divisiveness that often permeates religious and social landscapes. The line, "we are so similar that only our mutual hatred gives us a sense of identity," encapsulates the irony of how artificial divisions often overshadow shared human experiences. The poem criticizes the systems and mindsets that perpetuate these divisions, describing how they give rise to conflicts, marginalization, and an undue focus on titles and roles rather than individual merit. It makes a compelling argument against pigeonholing people into categories—be they religious, professional, or social—and calls into question the societal structures that support such divisions. This work offers a biting critique of how we view and treat one another, urging the reader to re-examine the paradigms we've come to accept.

"Besieged Warrior" offers a poignant commentary on national identity and the arbitrary, often perilous lines that divide us. It challenges the reader to question what defines a patriot, a traitor, or even an individual, when a "borderline" becomes the judge.

The book, beautifully translated into English by Shivam Tomar, is a precious gift to English readers and a great service to Hindi literature. Read this book to explore, to question, and most importantly, to feel the contemplative, soul-stirring experience that will leave you questioning long-held beliefs and seeing the world anew.

Kalpna Singh-Chitnis
Poet, Filmmaker, Editor – Life and Legends
Greater Los Angeles
29 / 8 / 2023

(Author of "Love Letters to Ukraine from Uyava," "Trespassing My Ancestral Lands," "Bare Soul," "Jo Tum Ho Wahi Hoon Main" and "Tafteesh Jari Hai.")

Translator's Note

For me, translating poetry is a bit like looking into a mirror and seeing myself in different lighting. Just as a mirror faithfully reflects what is without adding or beautifying, my goal in translating the poems in this collection was to capture the true feelings and essence of the original poetry. However, sometimes, my own reflection seems strange, much like the feeling when reading a translated poem. The words may change, the rhythm may shift, yet the core emotions can hit me in surprising ways.

I've come to realize that subtle nuances and cultural references in a translated poem can easily be missed. So, translating poems rooted in everyday language and dialects can sometimes be quite challenging, to the point where we had to leave out a few poems because their translation would have turned them into entirely new poems. Translating may seem simple when dealing with a straightforward poem where a literal translation works, but to truly test your translating skills, there exist a thousand poems or more.

It wouldn't have been possible without the humbleness of the poet these poems belong to. Two people from very different backgrounds and with a significant age gap can become great friends if the older one is genuinely modest, just like Kumar Mukul. Despite his extensive knowledge gained over years in journalism and writing, Kumar Mukul interacted with me with great humility. Translating his work brought me immense joy, and it was equally satisfying to see his warm welcome of young newcomers stepping into the challenging world of literature. The responsibility of translating his finest works, entrusted to me, felt like an honor I sincerely worked to fulfill.

When translating poems feels like writing your own, the task becomes easy. As someone who finds comfort in nature, whether it's the beauty of mountains, the sight of stars and the moon, or sitting quietly by the sea whenever the opportunity arises, I had the privilege of working on some of the most beautiful poems that blend human existence with the grandeur of nature.

The wide range of subjects within his poems often had me reaching out to him for a better understanding, and at times, I couldn't help but feel a bit embarrassed about my own limited knowledge. However, his boundless generosity always put me at ease.

Kumar Mukul's unwavering belief in poetry's power to untangle even the most complex ideas becomes clear in his exploration of subjects like international relations, the hidden motives and propaganda of the modern world, capitalism, and the manipulation of people based on religion. He skillfully weaves everyday aspects of life into his poems, using common objects to convey profound messages.

I faced significant challenges while translating some of the poems. I believe that reading a poem as a reader and as a translator are different experiences. A reader can interpret it in their own way, which may differ from what the poet intended, while the translator's job is to get as close as possible to what the poet must have wanted to convey. When the poet is just a ring away from you, it becomes easier, although many times, I felt hesitant about asking my simple questions, fearing it would make me look like someone who doesn't know much. But Kumar Mukul welcomed my interpretations while also explaining the core idea of a poem.

Long poems often have many paths leading to the main idea of the poem, providing a deeper understanding and more context. Short ones are the ones that sometimes made me doubt my translation. Languages have their own magic, but they have different ways of presenting it. The charm of everyday language and dialects often gets lost in translation. So, when I found it hard to capture the actual impact of a poem, I took some creative freedom to play with words instead of translating them literally.

I won't discuss any specific poem here. As a translator, I can only say so much, but as an enthusiastic admirer of his poetry, I find myself continually drawn to the poems featured in this collection. While maintaining a necessary level of objectivity, it's hard not to be captivated. Within this collection, you'll find some of the most beautiful love poems, presented in a way that's both eloquent and captivating. Kumar Mukul seamlessly transitions between philosopher and journalist, delving into profound truths hidden within significant concepts. The titular poem, "Poetry Decides," perfectly captures the essence of this anthology.

Now, as you hold this book in your hands, my sincere hope is that I have built a bridge between two languages, allowing these magnificent poems to cross effortlessly and touch the hearts of readers with ease.

Shivam Tomar

The Best Letters

The best letters are not necessarily those
with the neatest handwriting
or the simplest language. Rather, the best letters
are the ones that are legible despite their messy script
and convey meaning even when read in haste.
While their words may be fuzzy but they still manage
to reflect a face.

The best letters aren't the ones that are timely received
and read right away but the ones that cause us to leap
with joy throughout the entire day, the ones we treasure
and keep to ourselves until we read them by lamplight
in the privacy of the evening.

The best letters are also the ones that are sent but never
reach us, the ones that we anticipate but are lost in transit,
the ones that can only be read in our dreams.

सबसे अच्छे खत

सबसे अच्छे ख़त वो नहीं होते
जिनकी लिखावट सबसे साफ़ होती है
जिनकी भाषा सबसे खफीफ होती है
वो सबसे अच्छे ख़त नहीं होते

जिनकी लिखावट चाहे गड्ड-मड्ड होती है
पर जो पढ़ी साफ़-साफ़ जाती है
सबसे अच्छे ख़त वो होते हैं
जिनकी भाषा उबड़-खाबड़ होती है
पर भागते-भागते भी जिसे हम पढ़ लेते हैं
जिसके हर्फ़ चाहे धुंधले हों
पर जिससे एक चेहरा साफ़ झलकता है
जो मिल जाते हैं समय से
और मिलते ही जिन्हे पढ़ लिया जाता है
वो ख़त सबसे अच्छे नहीं होते
सबकी नज़र बचा जिन्हें छुपा देते हैं हम
और भागते फिरते हैं जिसकी ख़ुशी में सारा दिन
शाम लैंप की रोशनी में पढ़ते हैं जिन्हें
वो सबसे अच्छे ख़त होते हैं
जिनके बारे में हम जानते हैं कि वे डाले जा चुके हैं
और जिनका इंतज़ार होता है हमें
और जो खो जाते हैं डाक में
जिन्हें सपनों में ही पढ़ पाते हैं हम
वे सबसे अच्छे ख़त होते हैं।

Patches of Moonlight

As I gaze at the moon,
I find myself unable to determine whether
I am happy or sad. Frustrated by this uncertainty,
I approach a child standing nearby and inquire
about the moon's whereabouts. Initially, the child
searches for his own shadow and then points to the sky.
He then gestures towards the illuminated patches
of moonlight on the ground,
leads me to the realisation that as we speak of the moon,
we essentially refer to things immersed in the moonlight.

चाँदनी का टीला

चांद को देखते हुए
मैं तय ही नहीं कर पाता
कि खुश हूँ या उदास
झुंझलाहट में
पास खड़े बच्चे से पूछता हूँ
बता तो चांद कहाँ है
पहले वह अपनी छाया देखता है
फिर इशारा करता है आकाश की ओर
और ज़मीन पर उभरे चांदनी के टीलों को दिखाता है
तब मुझे लगता है
कि चांद की बात करते हुए हम
चांदनी में डूबी चीज़ों की बात करते हैं।

Poetry Decides

Poetry isn't meant to put ourselves
into the spotlight, but to tell what it is like
to be a human in words.
If you wish to know more, let me tell you
How it begins on a lover's lips,
blooms on the branches of Gulmohar,
and comes to rest on the blood-stained roadside.

Poetry can yield a harvest of bread,
It bridges the person and the public.
With a little understanding of the world,
Poetry is born, a proof that we are.
Understanding this world, even
in modest ways, grants us value
and gives rise to poetry as a proof
of our existence.

Poetry is the act of restlessly becoming someone else in our
verses. It tells that indifference is a mere mask,
hiding the vulnerability of the weak, while nurturing
empathy, is vital for our growth.

Poetry marries the smell of mango buds to the songs
of cuckoos in spring, shows us how a lover's cheeks
quiver when kisses are planted into the void.

It teaches us that even neon lights cannot banish
the darkness within, that distance is no barrier

when we travel at the speed of light or sound,
and that oneness is not just a pile of dead earthworms
but a tight-knit bond.

It imparts the wisdom to discern wolves from lambs
through the crosshairs. Poetry decides when to turn
the fire in our hearths into guiding torches.

Poetry is a force that can untangle knots where
others fail and it is present wherever there is
movement and life.

कविता तय करती है

जानते हुए कि कविता
व्यक्तित्व चमकाने की चीज नहीं
एक मुकम्मल बयान और शब्दों में
आदमी होने की तमीज है
जानना चाहोगे तुम
कि कविता क्या है
कैसे यह महबूबा के होठों से
गुलमोहर की शाखों पर खिलती हुई
सड़क पर बिखरे
आदमी के खून तक का सफर पूरा करती है
कविता रोटी की फसल पैदा कर सकती है
यह व्यक्ति को सार्वजनिक करती है
या सार्वजनिक को व्यक्त ?

अपनी छोटी सी समझ से
हम हैं, इसी से कविता है
यह हमारे होने का प्रमाण है
कविता मैं से
तुम या वह होने की छटपटाहट है
बतलाती है यह कि तटस्थता
नपुंसकों की अक्षमता ढकने को
एक सुंदर भावबोध है

और समष्टि से संलग्नता
उर्वर होने की शर्त

यह वसंत से
कोयल की कूक और बौरों की गंध का
संबंध साबित करती है
यह बतलाती है कि कैसे
शून्य में दागे गए चुंबनों के चिन्ह
प्रिया के रुखसारों पर सिहरन पैदा करते हैं
यह सिखलाती है
कि नियॉन लाइट्स की रौशनी
हमारे अंतर का अंधकार
दूर नहीं कर सकती
कि ध्वनि या प्रकाश के वेग से दौड़ें हम
धरती लंबी नहीं होने को
कि एकता मरे बेजान केचुओं का
समूह नहीं एक बंधी हुई मुट्ठी है

यह बंदूक की नली से
भेड़िए और मेमने का
फर्क करना सिखलाती है
कविता तय करती है कि कब
चूल्हे में जलती लकड़ी को
मशाल की शक्ल में थाम लिया जाए

या अन्य ढेर सारी गांठें
जिन्हें कोई नहीं खोलता
कविता खोलती है
जहाँ कहीं भी गति है वहीं जीवन है
और कविता भी।

Mountains

Why are we drawn towards mountains,
even though gravity resides within the Earth?
Wherever I look, I see people
being drawn towards them.

Clouds drift towards the mountains,
even if it means they must burst into rain,
colliding with them.
The wind embarks on a journey to the mountains,
only to graze against their slopes
and find its path altered.
The sun races to reach the mountains
before all else, striving to cast light
upon their darkest peaks.

Even the radiant moonlight seeks refuge
among the mountains,
though sometimes veiled by a touch of mist.

Yet, observe those trees,
ascending skyward,
yearning to reach the mountains,
to anchor themselves there.

Anyone can climb a mountain,
but only those with roots deep enough
to penetrate their stony hearts

and reduce them to dust
can truly endure.

If you try to soar like a cloud
towards the mountains,
you will be repelled,
just as a river is
with but a handful of sand.

पहाड़

गुरूत्वाकर्षण तो धरती में है
फिर क्यों खींचते हैं पहाड़
जिसे देखो
उधर ही भागा जा रहा है

बादल
पहाड़ों को भागते हैं
चाहे
बरस जाना पड़े टकराकर
हवा
पहाड़ को जाती है
टकराती है ओर मुड़ जाती है
सूरज सबसे पहले
पहाड़ छूता है
भेदना चाहता है उसका अंधेरा
चांदनी वहीं विराजती है
पड़ जाती है धूमिल

पर
पेड़ों को देखो
कैसे चढ़े जा रहे
जमे जा रहे
जाकर

चढ़ तो कोई भी सकता है पहाड़
पर टिकता वही है
जिसकी जड़ें हों गहरी
जो चट्टानों का सीना चीर सकें
उन्हें माटी कर सकें

बादलों की तरह
उड़कर
जाओगे पहाड़ तक
तो
नदी की तरह
उतार देंगे पहाड़
हाथों में मुटठी भर रेत थमा कर।

Left Hand

As I recline and read, my left hand gracefully
turns the pages, while my right hand delicately
holds the book. When my pen pauses, it signals
my lips to blow air into it, as if believing that
the sentiments reside within the ink. Resting on
my chin, my left hand remains still, observing
the moving pen, while my right hand continues
to write, oblivious to its surroundings.

During sleep, my right-hand rests upon my forehead,
assuming a philosopher's pose, while my left hand
lies nearby, like an inexperienced lover. When an itch
arises, my left hand swiftly attends to the affected spot.
When needed, it intertwines with my right hand, providing
comfort, and eventually, they both drift into slumber.

In moments of argument, my right hand is quick
to seize collars, while my left hand instinctively turns
to prayer, beseeching God in fear. Mechanically,
my right-hand salutes the boss, while my left hand
feels embarrassed, attempting to conceal itself.

Meeting friends, my left hand feels remorseful,
while my right hand continues to wave goodbyes.

It is my right hand that shows affection by caressing cows.
However, when it comes to milking cows or society,

my right hand always pulls along my left. My left hand
diligently assists my right hand in cleaning up the mess,
and later extends a handkerchief from its pocket.

Occasionally, my left-hand asserts that no task can be
accomplished without it, be it rope-weaving, wielding a shovel,
using a pistol, or lifting weights.

One day, recognizing the courage within my left hand,
I entrusted it with a pen, asking it to compose love poems
with its trembling fingers. Yet, it produced only illegible
scribbles, looking like the crow's feet my right hand
used to draw when I was a child.

When I offered a slate and pencil, my left hand complained
of the weight and refused to hold them. I advised it to rest
the slate on the ground, and as for itself, to cross its legs,
sit down, and continue writing.

1990, After reading a poem by Mangalesh Dabral

नेटरा हाथ

लेटा पढता होता हूँ
तो किताब उठाये रखता है दाहिना
और हल्के थामे नेटरा
पलटता चलता है पन्ना
लिखते लिखते रूक जाती है कलम
तब होंठों को सुसराता है नेटरा
जैसे जानता हो किधर छुपे हैं भाव
फिर कलम सरकते
ठुड्डी से अड़ देखता है निस्पंद
लिखते दाहिने को
जैसे खबर ही ना हो कुछ
सोते चिंतक की मुद्रा में
माथे पर पड़ा होता है दाहिना
तब नेटरा लेटा रहता है
अनपढ़ प्रिया सा पास ही
कहीं सुरसुरी होती तो सहलाता
फिर दाहिने की अंगुलियों में
अंगुलियां फंसा
मनौवल करता सा सो जाता

झगड़ा झांटी में
लपक लेता दाहिना
कॉलर किसी का

तो अनहोनी के भय से कांपता नेटरा
विनती करने लगता ईश्वर से
बॉस को यंत्र सा
सैल्यूट दागता दाहिना
तो शर्म आती नेटरे को
और बगल छिपने की कोशिश करता वह

मित्रों से भेंट बखत
पछताता नेटरा
विदा की बेर भी
उछल उछल देर तक
हाथ हिलाता दाहिना ही
बछड़े की पीठ भी वही सहलाता

पर गाय दूहना हो या समाज
नेटरे को घसीट लेता साथ वह
सारी गंदगी साफ कराता उसी से
और थमा देता रूमाल
लो पड़े रहो लिपटे बांयी जेब में

कभी तो चुनौती ही दे देता नेटरा
कि रस्सी बंटने से बेलचा चलाने तक
बंदूक थामने से बोझ उठाने तक
है कोई काम जो हो बगैर नेटरा के

एक दिन मुझे लगा
कि दम है नेटरा में
तो पकड़ा दिया कलम
कि उतारे प्रेमगीत कोई
बिचकती अंगुलियों से

तब बना दिये उसने
कौए के टांग कई

बचपन में जैसा
लिखा करता था दाहिना

तब साहूकार से
लाया सिलेट पिनसिन
पकड़ाया नेटरा को
भारी भारी सा
लग रहा था उसे
कि बहाना कर रहा था वह
मैंने समझाया
भारी है
तो रख दो जमीन पर
और लिखो
पालथी मार कर लिखो।

1990, **मंगलेश डबराल** *की एक कविता पढ़कर।*

Morning

Unveiling the moonlight's mysteries,
Dawn emerges. Wake up,

with dew and dust on your feet,
embark on a journey. Witness

the world, though memories hold
night jasmine at its peak. It

may have grown weary from
its nightly vigils. Appreciate

and preserve its fragrant essence.
Wake up, while dogs sleep,

birds soar to new horizons.
Wake up and enter the dreams of children.

सुबह

चांदनी की
रहस्यमयी परतों को दरकाती
सुबह हो रही है

जगो
और पाँवों में पहन लो
धूल मिट्टी ओस
और दौड़ो
देखो-स्मृतियों में
कोई हरसिंगार अब भी हरा होगा
पूरी रात जग कर थक गया होगा
संभालो उसे-उसकी गंध को संभालो
जगो
कि कुत्ते सो रहे हैं अभी
और पक्षी खोल रहे हैं
दिशाओं के द्वार
जगो
और बच्चों के स्वप्नों में
प्रवेश कर जाओ।

Van Gogh's Ursula

"Do I need to marry every person I fall in love with?" Ursula
frustratingly questions before storming off and calling Vincent a
foolish redhead.

Mornings have always been moist yet burning with energy, while
evenings are always lovely, but with a tinge of sadness.

Love emerges, breaking through layers of soil, unleashing sprouts
that gaze into the unknown, playfully running amok. It tidies
tangled locks with gentle kisses, wipes away perspiration with a
scarf, leaving the rigid structure of language in awe of its endless
discussions.

Like a small bird testing its wings, love is filled with uncertainties
that we either strive to preserve or suppress. We often desire to
build walls, shielding it from the chaos of the world, unaware
that love is a powerful aspiration capable of breaking through
barriers and defenses.

Ultimately, we persist in our pursuit of love while battling to
survive, but sometimes the dream of waking up from slumber
shatters.

Every Vincent has an Ursula who sees him as crazy, blunt, and
foolish. It is Vincent who regards his thoughts as his beloved,
believing that his ideas hold greater significance than his own
sense of self-worth. Vincent is the one who makes and breaks

promises, wandering from door to door burdened by the greatest absurdities.

Throughout history, teachers have been won over by offering them accommodation and food. Even now, what does a Vincent truly need? Remembrance comes at no cost.

Yet, remembrance extracts a lifetime—a life that crumbles before our eyes, dissolving into fading sighs.

Love, as Isadora says, afflicts the soul rather than the body. It's a fever that consumes flaws, transforming lovers into warriors, and priests into scholars. It ignites vibrant eyes and electrifies language. Within every Vincent, an Ursula awakens, inspiring beautiful prayers and melodies.

Even the cruelest dictators harbor a fading Ursula within themselves.

Sometimes, this fever breaks, but by then it's too late. True conviction morphs into hollow whims.

In their resolve to preserve Ursula, they inadvertently kill her within themselves.

To Vincent, Ursula embodied a radiant blue-eyed joy, reminiscent of those rare mornings that leave an everlasting imprint. Yet, when the elusive light of the world blinds us, and we yearn for a glimmer hidden within, it flickers—evoking tangible pain at our inability to transform those golden moments into the cycles of morning and evening light.

Vincent contemplates Jesus, realizing that books offer profound and captivating discoveries. Despair cannot exist without hope. When Ursula loses herself in the book of life, she resurrects in Vincent's blood, his gaze, and his gestures. She is then recreated on canvases repeatedly, assuming diverse forms that are more authentic than the original.

वॉन गॉग की उर्सुला

क्या
हर प्यार करने वाले से
शादी करनी होगी मुझे
पूछती है–उर्सुला
और भाग खड़ी होती है
विन्सेंट को पुकारती
लाल सिर वाला बेवकूफ़

सुबहें होती आई हैं
शबनम से नम
और आग से भरी हुई
हमेशा से
और शामें
उदास-ख़ूबसूरत

गुलाम हो चुकी भाषा के व्याकरण को
अपनी बेहिसाब जिरहों से लाजवाब करता
मिट्टी की परतें तोड़
फेंकता अंकुर आज़ाद
कि ख़ब्तख़याली के
टकटकी बांधता, खिलखिलाता, भागता
बदहवास
बिखरती लटें संवारता, चुंबनों से
दुपट्टे से पसीना पोंछता
आता है प्यार -
चूजे-सा पर तोलता
भरता आशंकाओं से

कि उसकी रक्षा या हत्या को
आतुर हो उठते हम
कि बाज-बखत
खड़ी करनी चाहते दीवार
उसे बचाने की
दुनियावी जद्दो-जहद से
इससे गाफ़िल कि वह ख़ुद
एक बुलन्द निगाह है -
दरो-दीवार को भेदती -
फिर अन्तत: चूक कर
दुहराते हैं हम - प्यार
और दुश्वार करते हैं जीना
और टूटता है एक सपना
नींद में जागे का।

हर विंसेंट की
एक उर्सुला होती है
उसे दीवाना-मुँहफट-सिरफिरा कह
उसके मुँह पर किवाड़ भेड़ती
और होता है वह
एक विन्सेंट ही
ख़्याल को सनम समझता
ख़ुद को
ख़्याल से भी कम समझता
प्रतिज्ञाएँ करता-तोड़ता
महान मूर्खताओं से चिढ़ता-चिढ़ाता उन्हें मुँह
भटकाता ख़ुद को दर-ब-दर

रहने और खाने की व्यवस्था पर
अध्यापक मिल जाते हैं हमेशा से
और आज भी
फिर क्या चाहिए था विन्सेंट को
याद करने के पैसे तो नहीं लगते

यादें तो बस
जीवन मांगती हैं
एक निगाह में

एक बैठती आह में
बिखरता जीवन।

इजाडोरा कहती है -
प्रेम
शरीर की नहीं
आत्मा की बीमारी है
यह ज्वर
जला डालता है सारे कलुष
प्रेमी बन जाते हैं
योद्धा-पादरी-शिक्षक
यह ज्वर भर जाता है
आँखों में चमक
भाषा में खुनक
फिर तमाम विन्सेंटों के भीतर
उनकी उर्सुलाएं जाग पड़ती हैं
बोलने लगते हैं वो
महान प्रार्थनाएं प्रयाण-गीत पाठ

दुनिया के क्रूरतम तानाशाह भी
अपने भीतर समेटते रहते हैं
एक बिखरती उर्सुला

कभी-कभी ज्वर टूटता है
तब तक देर हो चुकी होती है
सच्ची जिंदें
बदल चुकी होती हैं
झूठी सनकों में

उर्सुला को बचाने की ज़िद् में वो
मार चुके होते हैं
अपने अंदर की उर्सुला को ही

जीवनानंद में नाचती
नीली आँखों का प्रकाश थी उर्सुला
विन्सेंट के लिए
उन कुछेक शामों-सुबहों की तरह
जो होते-बीतते

बैठ जाती हैं चुपके से भीतर
फिर जब दुनिया का मायावी प्रकाश
चौंधियाता है हमें
तो खो जाते हैं हम
कहीं भीतर दुबके
प्रकाश-पल की तलाश में
टिमटिमाता रहता है जो–अविच्छिन्न
एक टीस की तरह
कि उन प्रकाश-पलों को फिर-फिर
बदला नहीं जा सकता
सुबहों व शामों के प्रकाशवृत्तों में

विन्सेंट याद करता है–ईसा को
कि हरेक चीज़ मिल जाती है
किसी भी क़िताब से
ज़्यादा सम्पूर्ण और सुन्दर रूप में

कि कोई भी दुख
बिना उम्मीद के नहीं आता

हाँ
सचमुच की उर्सुला जब
खो जाती है कहीं
ज़िन्दगी की क़िताब में
तब
जीवित होने लगती है वह
विन्सेंट के लहू में-
निगाह में उसकी
उसके इशारों में-
फिर-फिर
रची जा रही होती है वह कैनवसों पर
मिथ्या आवरणों के भीतर
अपने मूल से भी
खरे रूप में।

11 September

It was their own towering forehead
that was collapsed at their feet,
causing them to flee in fear.

In that moment, their sole desire
was to escape their furrowed brows
and the cosmic fury of their own inner sight.

It was neither Hiroshima-Nagasaki,
nor Vietnam-Iraq,
but their own voracious, mighty hands
that smashed against their own faces.

They possessed their own arsenal,
with gunpowder originating from
their own factories.
They dug their own trenches,
yet ladders fell short,
leaving their feet submerged
 in the waters of helplessness.

Newton's third law of motion,
which they had sold numerous times,
now manifested within their own abode,
consequences of their own actions.

They possessed their own all-seeing eye,
cameras that belonged to them,
capturing and revealing everything to the world.
They had documented countless tragedies,
and today they witnessed that footage themselves.

ग्यारह सितंबर

यह उनका अपना ही विशाल माथा था
जो भरभराकर ढहा आ रहा था
ख़ुद उन्हीं के क़दमों में
और भयाक्रांत भाग रहे थे वे
भाग जाना चाह रहे थे
अपने ही माथे की तनी भृकुटी से
व अपनी ही तीसरी आँख के
वैश्विक प्रकोप से

हिरोशिमा-नागासाकी नहीं था वह
वियतनाम-इराक भी नहीं था
यह उनका अपना ही
सर्वग्रासी, महाबलशाली हाथ था
जो अपना ही मुँह जाब रहा था

उनके ही हथियार थे
बारूद भी उनके ही कारखानों की थी
उनकी अपनी ही खोदी खाइयाँ थीं
और मीनारों तक गढ़ गई थीं
और उनके पाँव
लाचारी के जलजले में
धँसे जा रहे थे

न्यूटन की गति का तीसरा नियम था यह
जिसे असंख्य बार बेच चुके थे वह
पर जो आज उनके ही घर में
लागू हो रहा था पहली बार
बिक रहा था उनके ही हाथों
उनकी अपनी ही सर्वद्रष्टा आँख थी
कैमरे भी उनके ही थे
जो दुनिया को सब-कुछ दिखा रहे थे

अनगिनत त्रासदियों को
फ़िल्मा चुके थे वे
आज वह फ़िल्म
वे ख़ुद देख रहे थे।

Politics

To truly live, you must stand firm,
Unyielding in your convictions.

Politics will demand compromise,
Urge you to surrender your freedom of mind,
To bow and become a bridge,
Enabling its passage across public dissent.

राजनीति

जिन्दा रहना हो
तो अडिग रहो

राजनीति चाहेगी
समझौता, स्वतंत्र विचारों की बलि
तुम्हारा झुकाव पुलों की तरह

जनाक्रोश पार जाने को।

Sadness

Amongst so many playful memories
Where shall I place
This sharp diamond of your sadness.

उदासी

ठिठोली करती
स्मृतियों के मध्य
कहाँ रखूँ
तुम्हारी उदासी का
यह धारदार हीरा।

Politician

The notion of change appears distant and superficial,
They seem unaffected by even the strongest fears.
They claim familiarity with the Gita's teachings,
Yet remain willing to harm their own populace.

They possess a keen awareness of your helplessness,
they know when you feel like laughing, your only refuge
is the shield of sarcasm.

राजनीतिज्ञ

विचलन तो दूर की बात है
डर की एक लौ भी नहीं छूती उन्हें
उन्होंने पढ़ रखी है गीता
वे मार सकते हैं स्वजनों को

वे जानते हैं तुम्हें
कि तुम लाचार हो कितने कि विनम्र हो
जो अक्सर हास्य
रीझे तो व्यंग्य कर सकते हो।

Moon's Jest

The moon is filled with resentment towards the lovers,
who come in search of it, yet become so engrossed
in each other that they fail to notice its presence above them.

In its exasperation, the moon playfully tickles
the grazing horses nearby, causing them to cease
eating and start whinnying, and when that fails to gain
attention, it incites the dogs to stir. The lovers momentarily
pause, and the moon experiences a brief relief
as they acknowledge its existence, only to be frustrated
again, as they are once more consumed by each other.

The moon then conceals stones beneath the grass,
but somehow, the lovers manage to traverse without stumbling.

Relentlessly, the moon pursues them until they reach
their home, then reluctantly withdraws the shadow
in a state of desperation.

Weary of waiting outside, the moon peeks through
the window, catching sight of them nestled together,
and quietly settles itself by the doorway.

मजाक चांद का

नामुराद प्रेमियों पर
बड़ा गुस्सा आता है चांद को
कि निकलते हैं वो चांद देखने के बहाने
पर आपस में ही तल्लीन हो जाते हैं ऐसे
कि याद ही नहीं रहता
कि ऊपर चांद भी है

ऐसे में चांद भी बाज नहीं आता है
पहले तो वह
मैदान में चरते घोड़ों को गुदगुदाता है
और वे चरना छोड़
लगते हैं हिन-हिनाने
और इससे भी बात नहीं बनती
तो उकसा देता है कुत्तों को

अब उठते हैं प्रेमी
और चांद ख़ुश होता है
कि चलो ख़याल तो आया
पर वे फिर आपस में गुम हो जाते हैं

चांद घास के नीचे तब
छुपा देता है पत्थर
पर गिरते-संभलते

बढ़ते ही जाते हैं वे
तब पीछे-पीछे
दरवाज़े तक
आता है चांद
और निराश हो
अपनी छाया वापिस ले लेता है
और बाहर खड़ा
इंतज़ार करता थक जाता है
तो झाँकता है खिड़की से
और पाता है
आपस में लिपटे वे सो रहे हैं
और वह भी वहीं
बिछ जाता है।

Sky

Holding up the sky on their branches,
How happy trees appear to be.

Let's join them in bearing the weight
and laugh together,
so that the sky may rise even higher.

आसमानों को

आसमानों को
फुनगियों पर उठाए
कैसे उन्मुक्त हो रहे हैं वृक्ष
आएँ
बटाएँ इनका भार
और मुक्त होकर हँसें
हँसें
ठहाके लगाएँ
हँसें
कि आसमान
कुछ और ऊपर उठ जाए।

Moon, on a rough day

In a freezing desolate night
while good people prepare for sleep,
the trees hold the threads of life,
while the moon tenderly cradles it.

Like a famished man
traversing the dream of a meal,
Like a stranger passing through a kind gaze,
I wander through the realm of moonlight
within the confines of my bed.

In this vast expanse where boys would have
played until darkness fell,
the moonlight continues to dance playfully
with the mist-soaked earth.

बेदिनी में चांद

ठिठुरती उजाड़ होती रात में
जब सुनागरिक सोने की तैयारी कर रहे होंगे
जीवन की डोर थामे खड़े हैं वृक्ष
चांद है कि इस डोर को हौले-हौले डुला रहा है
भूखा जैसे भोजन के सपने से गुज़र रहा हो
या नामालूम-सा कोई व्यक्ति
किसी की मीठी निगाह से
अपनी इस बेदिनी में मैं भी
चांदनी के ख़्वाबगाह से गुजर रहा हूँ
इस बड़े मैदान में
जहाँ शाम तक लड़के खेल रहे होंगे
कुहासे में भीगे मिट्टी के टीलों से
अभी चांदनी खेल रही है।

Tragedies

Why are tragedies so captivating,
drawing us in with fascination?

How can someone's pain
become so enticing to many,
that they start humming it in
every tune they know?

दुख

इतने हँसमुख क्यों होते हैं दुख
कि प्यार आने लगे उन पर

एक का दुख कैसे भा जाता है सबको
कि गाने लगते हैं सब उसको
एक दो-तीन सात सुरों में।

My Feet

Concealing the tangles of my awareness beneath
the soles of my shoes, these are my feet.
On dimly lit streets, while my frightened soul
remains behind, my feet venture ahead, taking
the first step.

मेरे पांव

चेतना की गुंजलकों को
तलुओं में छुपाए
ये मेरे पाँव हैं
अंधेरी राहों में जब
मेरी सहमी आत्मा
पीछे छूट जाती है
सबसे पहले
ये ही उठाते हैं क़दम।

The River and the Bridge

Even when the river runs dry,
a bridge remains a bridge.

A river of sand is still called
a river.

As long as this bridge exists,
the river perseveres,
awaiting the change in season.

नदी और पुल

नदी में पानी नहीं
फिर भी यह पुल
पुल है

रेत की नदी भी
नदी कहलाती है

जबतक यह पुल है
नदी रहेगी
मौसमों का इंतजार करती हुई।

Soul, a flicker

The soul flickers, if only one has
the vision to perceive it.

It embodies the chaos of our conscience.

Water surges, extending beyond its shore,
cleansing our skin.

Immortality is a distant dream
if only we could step into its embrace.

Otherwise, the soul is nothing more than
a heap of dry soil, vulnerable to being
carried away by the wind at its will.

And immortality–the very soul of that heap.

एक कौंध है आत्मा

एक कौंध है आत्मा
बशर्ते कि तुम्हारे पास निगाह हो

हलचल है अंतरमन की

कि छलकता चला आता है जल

किनारे के पार
भिंगोता त्वचा

और अमरता

एक स्वप्न है

अगर हमारे पास कदम हों
उधर बढ़ाने को

नहीं तो
मिटटी का सूखा ढेर है आत्मा
जिसे हवा जब चाहे उड़ा सकती है
और अमरता
उस ढेर की आत्मा।

How beautiful

How beautiful it is
to silently observe
the world as it goes on
being itself.

कितना अच्छा है

कितना अच्छा है
चुप रहना
बस देखते जाना
दुनिया को दुनिया होते।

If this is religion, then what defines hell?

Is it religion
that, without touching your soul,
judges your worth
by the clothes you wear?

Is it religion
that pursues you like a wolf
and compels you to seek refuge
from door to door?

Is it religion that wields weapons
to harm you
but offers no shelter?

Is it the might of religion
that, when it aims to harm you,
leaves no room for salvation?

If this is religion,
then what defines hell?

यह धर्म है, तो नर्क क्या है ?

क्या यह धर्म है
जो आपकी आत्मा का तो स्पर्श नहीं करता
पर आपके शरीर को ढकने वाले कपड़ों से
आपकी अहमियत तय करता है
जो भेड़िए की तरह आपका पीछा करता है
जिससे बचने को आप
दर ब दर भागते फिरते हैं

क्या यह धर्म है
जो हथियार धारण करता है
आपको नेस्त-नाबूद करने को
पर आपकी रक्षा के कोई सूत्र
नहीं हैं जिसके पास

क्या यह धर्म की ताकत है
कि अगर वह
आपकी हत्या पर उतर आए
तो कोई आपको बचा नहीं सकता

यह धर्म है
तो नर्क क्या है?

For some light years

My light will keep reaching you
for countless light-years,
even when I cease to exist.

As you quest to find its origin,
when you reach the ultimate end,
I'll be a black hole long-formed.

At that juncture in time,
you'll find yourself unable to reach me
or return anywhere
within this boundless universe.

कुछ प्रकाशवर्षों तक

कुछ प्रकाशवर्षों तक
पहुंचती रहेगी
मेरी रोशनी
तुम तक
तब भी
जब
नहीं रहेगा मेरा अस्तित्व

उस रोशनी को ढूंढती
जब
पहुंचोगी मंजिल तक
मैं बदल चुका हूँगा
एक ब्लैक होल में

फिर
तुम
ना पहुंच सकोगी मुझ तक
न
वापिस जा सकोगी
कहीं भी
इस असीम ब्रह्मांड में।

River (I)

Upon meeting her after a lengthy separation,
my presence ripples in her eyes.
The depths of her gaze draw me in,
first to my knees,
then my waist,
until finally,
my shoulders submerge,
and I let myself immerse in her embrace.

And now, I am holding her closely.

In the end,
with a breath held tight,
I completely submerge.

नदी - एक

अरसा बाद
मिल रहा था उससे
मेरा वर्तमान कांप रहा था
उसकी आंखों में
गहराइयां
खींच रही थीं उसकी
सो
उतरता चला गया
ठेहुने-कमर-कंधे
और अब
गले लग रहा था उसके

अंत में
सांसें रोक
डुबकियां लगा दी मैंने।

River (II)

I yearned to immerse myself
in her presence, yet time and again,
I found myself lost in her memories.

frustratingly, she would snatch
the ground beneath my feet,
and though I attempted
to find balance, I was pulled
into the sorrows of the past.

Finally, a tide rolls in,
A feeling of unease washes over me,
My breath starts to swell,
It's all present now, surging
Abundantly through every vein within me.

नदी - दो

उतरना तो मैं
उसके वर्तमान में
चाह रहा था
पर
बार - बार
चला जा रहा था
स्मृतियों में उसकी
परेशान हो
अपनी जमीन
खींच ले रही थी वह
बार-बार
मैं संभलता
फिर बहने लगता
अतीत की रौ में
आखिर
एक ज्वार आया
और उब-चूब होने लगा मैं
सांसें
फूलने लगीं
और अब वर्तमान ही वर्तमान था
भिगोता
रग-रग।

First Love

At times, it shone as brightly as an eye, sparkling
In the middle of a sunny day, other times
Like the first face we see emerging
On a misty morning in January.

One fateful morning, it showed up unexpectedly,
Softly knocking on my door, and when
I opened it, it barged right in, acting
Like it owned the place, left me feeling
Like a guest in my own home,
Permanently out of place for the rest of my life.

पहला प्यार

कभी वह दोपहर की धूप के मुक़ाबिल
आंखों की चमक की तरह था
तो कभी जनवरी के घने कुहासे वाली
सुबहों से निकलते पहले चेहरे की तरह

निपट अकेली एक सुबह
उसने कुंडी खड़काई
दरवाजा खुला तो यूँ भीतर आया
जैसे उसका ही घर हो
और उम्र भर को बेघर कर गया।

Killers

Despite all the attacks, Israel is willing
To send the coronavirus vaccine to Palestine.

Are killers lenient towards other killers today,
Or is leniency one of the pawns on the killer's chessboard?

What a time it is when murderers are rising
To power all around the world.

Biden calls Putin a 'murderer' from afar,
But when they meet, gives him a pair
Of gold glasses as a gift.

At the behest of Biden, proud Putin states
That it doesn't matter to him who calls him what!"

हत्यारे

मन भर
बम बरसाने के बाद
इजरायल का प्रधान
फिलिस्तीन को
कोरोना का टीका
भेंट करना चाहता है

हत्यारे
हत्यारों के प्रति
उदार हैं आज
या कि उदारता
हत्यारों की शतरंज का
मोहरा है

यह कैसा समय है
जब दुनिया भर में
हत्यारे
प्रधान हुए जा रहे

बाइडेन
पुतिन को 'हत्यारा' कहता है
और मिलकर उसे
सोने का चश्मा भेंट करता है

बाइडेन के कहे पर
इतराता
पुतिन कहता है
के इससे
उसे कोई अंतर नहीं पड़ता
कि कौन उसे क्या कहता है !

Will keep listening to you

Till your picture
speaks,

I will keep listening
to you.

तुझे सुनता रहूँगा मैं

तेरी तस्वीर
जब तक
बोलती है

तुझे
सुनता रहूँगा
मैं।

A Small Bird

When a small bird began to burn
From the scorching sun's heat,
It lifted its head abruptly and spat
On it fiercely, hoping to put out the flames.

I'm not sure if it made much of a difference
To the Sun, but it certainly didn't sit well
With its descendants. As a result,
They grabbed their weapons and started chasing

After the disrespectful bird. The little bird
Started fleeing from one world to another,
Trying to save its life. Who will protect her?
The stars speculate that only God can save her,

But where can one find God? Everyone believes
The bird's chances of survival are slim.
The cameras on every planet are focused
On the bird, waiting for it to succumb

And perish, so they can create a sensational
Story out of it, filling a void in the news
That has been empty for so long.

For Tasleema Nasreen, 1988

चिड़िया का बच्चा

एक चिड़िया का बच्चा जब
सूरज की तपिश से जलने लगा
तो जाने क्या सूझी उसे
कि बुझा देने की नीयत से
सर उठाकर उस पर थूक दिया

अब सूरज की सेहत पर इसका क्या असर पड़ा
पता नहीं
पर उसके वंशधरों को यह नागवार गुजरी
सो अस्त्र-शस्त्र ले पड़ गये उसके पीछे
अब आफत की मारी वह नन्हीं सी जान
लगी भागने इस लोक से उस लोक
उसे कौन शरण देगा
चांद तारे आपस में बतिया रहे हैं
कि इसे बस खुदा ही बचा सकता है
अब खुदा को कोई कहाँ ढूँढ़े

सबका ऐसा विश्वास है

कि चिड़िया का बचना मुश्किल है
ग्रहों के कैमरे चिड़िया पर नजर टिकाये हैं
कि चिड़िया मरे कि एक
हेडलाइन न्यूज तैयार हो
जिसकी जगह अभी खाली है।

1988 , तसलीमा नसरीन के लिए

Love

On the outskirts of my memories,
glitters a star

Its shimmering light washes over
The galaxies within my mind.

It might fall apart tomorrow,
dispersing its frigid dust in all directions

Or it can transform itself into dark space
making me non-existent.

प्यार

स्मृतियों के सीमांत पर
टिमटिमाता तारा
अपनी कांपती रौशनी की
अंतरलय से
मानस की आकाशगंगाओं को धोता हुआ
कल को
बिखर भी सकता है
छिटकाता
दिशाओं में अपनी शीतल धूल
या
बदल सकता है
खुद को
ब्लैक स्पेस में
मुझे अनस्तित्व करता हुआ।

Love, Two Poems

1

Love lights up the mornings
and nights, filling them with
an air of mystique. In love, stars

begin to chime, and the moonlight,
dormant all day, resurfaces
with newfound glow. In love,

our spirit seems detached
within its own self, yearning
to be somewhere else. Love sends

waves of bliss so high across
the visible horizon that the sky
gets engulfed by the sea. With
its fragrant blue essence, it evokes
the boundless saltwater of the ocean,
illuminating it. In love, we sense
an infinite string of words ready
to spring forth from the heart at any
moment, capable of melting even
the heart of stones.

Seven hues spread across the bright
sky, nourishing and rejuvenating
the feathers of birds. The night, weary

from tending to the intoxicating
Harsingars throughout the night,
surrenders to the morning, filled
with a fragrant embrace.

Two unknown people become grand
in love, eclipsing all myths and legends
that existed before them. Love, a faint,

desperate cry that keeps getting louder,
making the galaxies shake, turning
the weary starlight into countless
points of lights.

2

Love is an eruption, that awakens
like a nightmare in troubled sleep.

Much like unending tides that break
the bones of the coast, love

relentlessly appears throughout life,
reducing people to miserable
and vulnerable beings. Love,

a humble rejection to the golden
camels of the global market, reminding
us that we are free and prosperous
with the warmth of our spirits. You may
continue borrowing words from us
indefinitely, without repayment, to refurbish
your luck.

Love, a unified advertisement of hearts
in anguish, affirming that yes,
we are alone, suffering, and hungry,
yet only we possess the power to fill

the world's boundless storehouses
and treasure chests. For, you cannot
trade our insatiable desire.

Love, Love, and Love.

The same sound echoes in all directions,
both within and outside the human body.

Love, love, and only love.

प्यार- दो कविताएँ

1

प्यार
आलोकित कर जाता है
सुबहों को
और शामों को
बनाता चला जाता है
रहस्यमयी

प्यार
जैसे तारों से आती है टंकार...
और सारा दिन निस्तेज पड़े
चांद की रौशनी
वापस आने लगती है

प्यार
कि आत्मा अपने ही शरीर से
बेरुख़ी करती
कहीं और जा समाने को
मचलने लगती है

प्यार
और ख़ुशियों का ठाठें मारता पारावार
चतुर्दिक

और आसमान डूबता चला जाता है
समंदर में
उसके अनंत खारेपन को
अपनी नीली सुगंध से रचता...
रौशन करता
कि शब्दों की अनंत लड़ी
फूटने-फूटने को होती है
जेहन से
और इस नाजुक लड़ी में
कैद होता चला जाता है
कोई भी कठोरतम हृदय

प्यार
और अरुणाकाश में
पसरने लगते हैं सप्तवर्णी रंग
पंछियों के परों को स्निग्ध
और ऊर्जामयी करते हुए

प्यार
और पूरी रात नशे में फूटते
हरसिंगारों को संभालती
थकने लगती है रात
और जा गिरती है
सुबह की गोद में
सुगंध से पूरित!

प्यार
और दो नामालूम से जन
एक दूसरे को
बनाना शुरू करते हैं विराट
तो फिर तमाम मिथकों
और दंतकथाओं को

उनका पार पाना
कठिन पड़ने लगता है
प्यार
एक धीमी-सी आकुल पुकार
जो बहुगुणित होती
कँपाने लगती है
आकाशगंगाओं को
और तारों की छीजती
बेचैन रौशनी
अनंत प्रकाश बिंदुओं में
तब्दील होती चली जाती है...

2

प्यार
जैसे एक हाहाकार
आकुल-व्याकुल जनों की
नींद में जगता
दु:स्वप्नों की तरह
जनसमुद्र की अनंत पछाड़
तोड़ती हाड़ तट का

प्यार
एक विनम्र इनकार
विश्वबाज़ार के सुनहले ऊँटों को
कि हम जो भी, जैसे भी हैं
स्वतंत्र और समृद्ध हैं
अपनी आत्मा के ताप के साथ

प्यार
कि हाँ तुम अब भी
ले सकते हो हमसे
अनंत उधार शब्दों का

और उसका मोल चुकाए बिना
उससे अपनी क़िस्मत
चमकाए फिर सकते हो

प्यार
पीड़ित जनों की आत्मा का
एकल और संयुक्त इशतहार कि
हाँ, हम अकेले हैं
पीड़ित हैं, क्षुधित हैं
पर हम ही भर सकते हैं
विश्व का अक्षय अनंत अन्न, रत्न कोश
कि हमारी असमाप्त क्षुधा का
तुम नहीं कर सकते ब्योपार...

प्यार
प्यार
प्यार
आदमी के अंदर और बाहर
दसों दिशाओं से आती है
एक ही पुकार
प्यार
प्यार
प्यार।

Truth-Lie

When you sense that truth is faltering
all around you

It's, in reality, the lies residing
within you that are slowly corroding
you from the inside.

सच-झूठ

जब तुझे लगे
कि दुनिया में सत्य
सर्वत्र हार रहा है

समझो
तेरे भीतर का झूठ
तुझको ही
कहीं मार रहा है।

Mountains, Six Poems

1.

During the different stages of life,
we often contemplate mountains, which,
despite their challenges, provide a peak
to briefly stand upon, untouched by
the grandeur of life's unfolding.

2.

When the cold wind grazes our bodies, mountains are brought to
mind. Nothing compares to memories; they mend all the mess as
soon as they touch us. A train's smoky exhale triggers a memory
of a girl. See, how strange can memories be! In memories,
mountains weigh as lightly as flowers and are equally magnificent.
Only in memories we can kiss mountains as the sky does.

3

I descend with the belief that moments
ago, I stood atop this mountain. Now,
as I gaze at it, I question if I truly
was there. Looking upwards, I ponder,
can one inscribe their name in the vastness
above, or would the stone beneath my feet
acknowledge any name at all?

As I continue my descent, the idea
of gathering some stones crosses my mind,

to preserve the sparkling memory
of these mountains. But can stones
ever be mountains?

4

I'm gasping, but with joy, having scaled
a mountain, yet now it's time to descend.

I contemplate, why do peaks exist?
They cannot offer anyone shelter. Clouds,
wind, and the sun, everything is here,
so why no roots? I wish I could turn
into stone right here, but it would take
millions of years.

5

Mountains, do you have hands?
Do you ever feel the urge to push
something down? You call to us from a distance,
offering comfort like a soft bed,
yet never prompting us to depart.
Even when we lament our descent halfway,
we still journey downward.
Do we fear that over time, you might expel us?
No, mountains would never commit such an act.
We persist in our descent with mixed emotions.

6.

How effortlessly these mountains embed
themselves in our memories, with
their dark green cliffs appearing even darker
in recollection, and their fountains of water,
both hot and cold. The mountains become
so light that they seem to sprint, but they
fail to realize that our memories are like mist,
not easily torn through like the wind.

Despite being filtered, these memories can
protect us. But how can you be so heartless
that when you find us alone, you rush to
rest upon our chest!

1997

पहाड़ : छह कविताएँ

1

जीवन के विस्तारों में
अक्सर याद आते हैं पहाड़
कि चाहे वे थकाते बहुत हैं
पर जल्द ही दे देते हैं कोई चोटी
जहाँ खड़े हो
क्षण भर को
तटस्थ हो सकें हम
विस्तारों के चक्रवर्तित्व से

2

उदी हवा शरीर से लगती है
तो सिहरते हुए याद आते हैं पहाड़
यादों का भी सानी नहीं
छूते ही बरोबर कर देती हैं ये विषमताओं को
अब इसमें क्या तुक कि धुआं छोड़ती रेल को देख
एक लड़की की याद आती है

यादों में पहाड़ का वजन
फूल से ज्यादा नहीं होता
ना ही फूलों से कम खूबसूरत लगते हैं पहाड़
यादों में संभव होता है
कि हम चूम सकें पहाड़ों को
जैसे उन्हें चूमता है आकाश

3

नीचे उतर आया हूँ पहाड़ों से
सोचता कि अभी चोटी पर था
चोटी को देखता हूँ तो लगता है
कि क्या सचमुच वहां था

उपर शून्य में कोई कैसे लिखे
कोई नाम
पांव तले की चट्टान भी
नाम स्वीकारेगी क्या

तब तोड़ता चलूँ पत्थर कुछ
टुकड़े चमकदार याद में
पर क्या पत्थर पहाड़ होते हैं

4

मारे खुशी के हांप रहा हूँ
चोटी चढ़ी है पहाड़ की
अब उतरना है नीचे

आश्रय नहीं दे पातीं
तो बनती क्यों हैं चोटियाँ

वहां बादल है हवा है सूरज है
पर जड़ें क्यों नहीं हैं
होता है यहीं पत्थर हो जाएं
पर लगेंगे करोड़ बरस

5

पहाड़ों क्या तुम्हारे हाथ नहीं होते
इच्छाएं नहीं होतीं चोटी से ढकेलने की

बुलाते हो दूर से सिर भी चढ़ाते हो
फिर उतरने क्यों नहीं कहते

पछताते हम ही उतरते हैं
कि उतरे क्यों
उतारे जाने का डर तो नहीं

नहीं ऐसा नहीं करोगे
यही सोचते खुश उदास होते
हम उतर आते हैं पर उतर पाते हैं

6

हो तो पहाड़
पर कैसी सफाई से
पैठ जाते हो स्मृतियों में हमारी
और भी गहरी काली हरी चट्टानें बनकर
और सोते गर्म ठंडे जल के

इतने हल्के हो जाते हो
कि लगाते हो दौड़
भूल जाते हो
कि धुंध सी ये स्मृतियां हैं हमारी
हवाएं नहीं कि चीरे चले जाओ

खुद छलनी हो जाएंगी ये
पर अगोरेंगी तुम्हें
पर कैसे बेरहम हो
अकेला पाते ही
होने लगते हो सवार छाती पर।

Place of a shovel

A bewildered worker and his wife
wander through the bustling streets
of the cyber-city.

The man carries a sturdy pointed
shovel resting upon his shoulder,
while a small trowel balances
on the woman's head.

In art galleries, my eyes would widen
at the sight of pots gracefully
perched upon women's heads.

How effortless!

If I were to encounter Kedarnath Singh
at this very moment, I might tell him
that a shovel's rightful place is not
within a drawing room, but rather
atop a moving head.

कुदाल की जगह

सायबर सिटी की व्यस्ततम सड़क पर
भटकता बढ़ा जा रहा था श्रमिक जोड़ा
आगे पुरुष के कन्धे पर
नुकीली, वज़नी, पठारी खंती थी
पीछे स्त्री के सिर पर
छोटी-सी पगड़ी के ऊपर
टिकी थी
स्वतन्त्र कुदाल

कला दीर्घाओं में
स्त्रियों के सर पर
कलात्मकता से टिके मटके देख
आँखें विस्फारित हो जाती थीं मेरी

पर कितना सहज था वह दृश्य
अब केदारनाथ सिंह मिलें
तो शायद मैं उन्हें बता सकूँ
कि कुदाल की सही जगह
ड्राइंगरूम में नहीं
एक गतिशील सर पर होती है।

What is Beauty

Who possessed greater beauty, Gandhi
or Socrates? And what about Madame Curie,
wasn't she beautiful as well?

"What truly defines beauty?" I inquire
of Alok da.

He whispers, as if in a trance —

*"The queens have faded away, their
memory no more valuable than a rusted
tin can.*

*The queens have faded away, yet the women
who once toiled across the expansive
horizon, still continue to reap the harvest."*

क्या है सुंदरता

क्या सुकरात सुंदर थे
या गांधी
मदाम क्यूरी क्या सुंदर थीं
आलोक दा से पूछा मैंने-
आखिर क्या है सुंदरता

पता नहीं, किस ट्रांस में जाकर
बोले वो -
"रानियाँ मिट गईं
जंग लगे टिन जितनी कीमत भी नहीं
रह गई उनकी याद की
रानियाँ मिट गईं
लेकिन क्षितिज तक फ़सल काट रही औरतें
फ़सल काट रही हैं।"

How beautiful we both are

She is concerned that her beauty has
diminished compared to before, and I, too,
acknowledge that I have lost my youthful
complexion.

Nostradamus predicted that by the year
2018, the world would lose its beauty,
and by the year 2025, there would be
only a handful of humans remaining.

Nevertheless, I hold the belief that after
2025, when we will be walking together
in a world devoid of others, the haunting
silence of that era will celebrate the
exquisite beauty within us both.

कि हम दोनों कितने सुंदर हैं

चिंतित है वह
कि पहले सी सुंदर ना रही
जानता हूँ मैं
कि पहले सा सुर्खरू ना रहा
भविष्यवाणी है नास्त्रेदमस की
के 2018 के बाद दुनिया
सुन्दर नहीं रह जाएगी
और 2025 के बाद
रह जायेंगे लोग गिनती के

पर सोचता हूँ मैं
कि 2025 के बाद के जनशून्य और
खाली-खुली दुनिया में
हम घूमेंगे साथ-साथ
हाथों में हाथ डाले

तब शायद
उस समय का दुनियावी सन्नाटा कहे
कि हमदोनों कितने सुंदर हैं।

Jyan Drez, the essence of Humanity

Amidst the presence of political opportunists
at every street intersection, grooming their
stained teeth with the remnants of democracy,
there remains an individual who chooses
to travel by foot to the tune of Jana-Gana-Mana.

'Jyan Drez', I may not comprehend
your two-word name, but I can hear
the sound of your bicycle.

Similar to the entire nation
that once followed Gandhi's
larger-than-life acts, we aspire
to walk alongside you.

Finally, after a considerable period,
someone's narratives waft through the air
like the essence of humanity.

Although the intricacies of your
and Amartya Sen's economics may seem
like an unfamiliar language to us,
your account of government officials
surreptitiously seizing land in cities
compared to the genuinely illegal slums
is as clear as water.

ज्यां द्रेज - जैसे, मनुष्यता की खुशबू

जहाँ हर चौक चौराहे पर
राजनीतिक हुंडार
अपनी रक्तस्लथ दाढ़
लोकतंत्र की राख से
चमकाते फिर रहे
कोई पांव-पैदल चल रहा
जन-गण-मन की धुन पर

'ज्यां द्रेज'
दो शब्दों का तुम्हारा नाम
मेरी समझ में नहीं आता
पर तुम्हारी सायकिल की टुन-टुन
सुन पा रहा मैं

जैसे
गांधी की
आदमकद हरकतों के पीछे
यह पूरा देश
भकुआया सा चल पड़ा था
हम चलना चाह रहे तुम्हारे साथ

बहुत दिन बाद
किसी के किस्से हवाओं में हैं
जैसे मनुष्यता की खुशबू

अमर्त्य सेन और तुम्हारा अर्थशास्त्र
नहीं पड़ता हमारे पल्ले
पर अवैध झुग्गियों के मुकाबले
महानगरों में कारों द्वारा
कब्जाई गई जमीनों का
तुम्हारा हिसाब स्पष्ट है।

East Wind

The East Wind flows absorbing
everything in the continuation
of its affectionate embrace.

The East Wind flows applying
the moist blue of the sky to its eye,
turning the inside out

letting the outside in.

हवा है यह

स्नेहिल आगोश की
निरंतरता में
समोती

पूरबा
हवा है यह

आकाश का
नम नीलापन
आंखों में आंजती
भीतर को करती बाहर
बाहर को भीतर भरती
हवा है यह।

Facebook, a self-criticism

With the same face
We confront one another
time and time again.

Now possessing eyes, yet lacking vision,
Our minds take flight from the keyboard
But fail to venture beyond the computer screen.

We may have less work
but more achievements to show for it

In this world full of ignorance
and misery, we stand facing one another,
Indifferent to most things, upholding
the culture of "after you."

फेसबुक
एक आत्मालोचना

अपना चेहरा उठाए
खड़े हैं हम बारहा
मुकाबिल आपके

अब आंखें हैं
पर दृष्टि नहीं है

मन हैं
पर उसकी उड़ान
की बोर्ड से कंपूटर स्क्रीन तक है

काम कम है हमारे पास
और उपलब्धियां हैं बेशुमार

जहालत और पीड़ा से भरे
इस जहान में
अपना चेहरा लिए
खड़े हैं हम

सबसे असंपृक्त

पहले आप
पहले आप की संस्कृति
संभालते हुए।

Jungles

In this wilderness of modern civilization,
some jungles will continue to exist
with their blind-womb cave-like solitude
and creaking of dry leaves.

They shall survive
much like a cactus does.

कोई जंगल

रह ही जाएगा
कोई जंगल
अंधी गर्भ गुफा और
सूखे पत्तों के चरमराते
अपने एकांत के साथ
आधुनिक सभ्यता के बियाबानों में
जैसे बच जाता है जीवट
नागफनी की तरह।

Death, an epigram

1.

O Death,
Who are you?
Where do you come from,
and where do you return to?

You pass by the mightiest of creatures,
observing them with the same impartiality
as you observe everyone else with.

2.

O Death,
Where do you reside?
Do you dwell within us,
or do you arrive from the outside
to bring an end to our lives?

3.

O Death,
Do you have a purpose?
How do you prefer to manifest?
With screams, wicked laughter,
performing *Tandava*,
or silently, like a virus,
lulling us into eternal slumber?

4.

O Death,
Are you a fleeting moment or a lifetime?
From the moment of our birth,
you begin accumulating your own age.

5.

O Death,
Are you heartless?
Or is your dread
an endless source of compassion?

6.

O Death,
We envision you as a deep abyss,
yet under the scorching sun,
you transform into a searing wave of heat
and afflict us much like
you do on a dark, chilling night.

7.

O Death,
How irresistible is your embrace,
that even Sita buries herself in the ground,
and Ram, consumed by the anguish
of separation from Lakshmana,
descends into the Sarayu without hesitation.

8.

O Death,
You always instill fear within us,
but how do you greet someone
who smiles
as they lift the poisoned cup
to their lips?

Poetry Decides
Kumar Mukul

9.

O Death,
Don't always loom over our heads
like a sword.
This mind, gripped by your profound terror,
often loses its sanity
and starts undermining you.

मृत्युसूक्त

(१-९)

(१)

हे मृत्यु,
कौन हो तुम
कहाँ से आती हो
चली जाती हो कहाँ ..
कैसे तुम, महाबली और बलि पशुओं को
समदृष्टि से निहारती गुजर जाती हो ?

(२)

हे मृत्यु,
कहाँ निवास है तुम्हारा
हमारे ही भीतर रहती हो तुम
या बाहर कहीं से आकर
हमारे जीव का हरण करती हो ?

(३)

हे मृत्यु,
क्या तुम्हारी कोई पुकार है
गर्जना, हहास और तांडव करती
आती हो तुम
या चुपचाप विषाणु सी प्रवेश कर
सुला देना पसंद है तुम्हें ?

(४)

हे मृत्यु,
तुम क्षण हो
या जीवन हो पूरा
जन्म लेते ही
समेटने लगती हो, अपनी उम्र ?

(५)

हे मृत्यु,
निष्करुण हो तुम
या तुम्हारा आतंक ही
अविरल स्रोत है, करुणा का ?

(६)

हे मृत्यु,
हम तुम्हें गहन अंधकार की तरह देखते हैं
पर तुम कड़ी धूप में लू की लहर बन
उसी तरह त्रस्त करती हो
जैसे कालरात्रि में शीतलहर बन ?

(७)

हे मृत्यु,
कैसे तुम हमें
अपनी आगोश में आने को
प्रेरित करती हो
कि राम को अश्रुपूरित नत्रों से देखती सीता
धरती में समा जाती हैं
और लक्ष्मण के वियोग में राम
उतर जाते हैं सरयू में ?

(८)

हे मृत्यु,
तुम सदा हमें भयाक्रांत करती हो
पर जब कोई मुस्कुराता हुआ
विष के प्याले को
अपने होठों से लगाता है
तब तुम उसका स्वागत कैसे करती हो ?

(९)

हे मृत्यु,
हर क्षण लटकती तलवार सी
सर पर टंगी मत रहा करो
गहरे आतंक से
यह सर
अक्सर फिर जाया करता है
जो तुम्हारी महत्ता को कम करता है !

For Meena Kumari

Pain resides not within your eyes
alone, but beneath our very skin.

The moment we catch a glimpse
of you, pain bursts forth,
one blister at a time.

मीना कुमारी के लिए

दर्द
तुम्हारी आंखों में नहीं
हमारी रगों में होता है

छू देती हैं निगाहें
उभर आता है दर्द
फफोले-फफोले।

Capitalists have taken hold of Cameras

Capitalists have taken hold of cameras—
Cameras as tiny as mischievous buttons
and as colossal as the necks of dinosaurs.

In turn, cameras have enslaved people,
all nearsighted, fixated on the scene
like slaves.

They are commanded to capture
whatever lies within the frame
that can be sold, without exception—
be it their mother, father, siblings,
friends, or daughter.

It is the future's objective and the present's
Demand that anything happening around
which can generate capital must be
captured.

Bear in mind the teachings of the Gita
that in this war called life,
there are no brothers or sisters;
there is only money,
and whatever favors its cause is righteous,
while the rest is worthless.

We will all turn to ashes by tomorrow,
so forget about yourself and savor
this moment.

You are merely a puppet in the hands
of destiny, called capitalism.

आज पूंजी ने पाल लिए हैं कैमरे

आज पूंजी ने
पाल लिए हैं कैमरे
भांति-भांति के
चुटपुटिया बटन से लेकर
डायनासोरों के गरदनों से विशाल

और कैमरों ने
पाले हैं मनुष्य
एक से
दूरदृष्टि दोष वाले
दृश्य पर नजर टिकाए
गुलाम

अब दृश्यो में जो भी हो
बिकाउ
अब वह चाहे उनके मां,बाप,भाई,बहन,प्रेमिका,बेटी
ही क्यों न हों

उन्हें आदेश है कि कैद करो
वर्तमान की मांग, भविष्य की मंजिल है यह

कि कैद करो
घटित होते हर उस दृश्य को
जो इजाफा करता हो पूंजी का

कि याद करो उपदेश गीता का
इस जीवन युद्ध में कोई बंधु-बांधव नहीं
बस पूंजी है
और इसमें सब जायज है
जो उसके पक्ष में है
बाकी निस्सार है सब
कल सबको मिल जाना है माटी में

बस यह क्षण
जिसमें घटित हो रहा यह दृश्य

इसे अमर कर देना है
खुद को भुलाकर
कि नियति के हाथ के खिलौने हो तुम
और तुम्हारी नियति है यह पूंजी ...।

Those who turn their back on life

The girl whom I briefly met at a gathering
later messages me,
and as we converse,
she confesses her particular fascination
with suicide victims.
I was uncertain of her true intentions
when she shared this with me.
Many of the individuals I admire
have also tragically taken their own lives—
Mayakovsky, Van Gogh, Marina,
and the poem "Mayakovsky" penned
just before his suicide
holds a captivating charm for me,
like *The Starry Night.*
However, I cannot bring myself
to end my own life.
A sense of unease envelops me
as I envision my severed head
resting upon a railroad track
besides my lifeless body.

But recently,
one of my friends committed suicide
by consuming sleeping pills.
He was as playful as I am.
Haha, am I still?

"I, too, once took sleeping pills,
yet somehow, I survived."

"Are you mad?"

"I was deeply distraught, sir.
I fell in love with a man
only to later discover
that he was married and engaged
in numerous extramarital affairs.
Meanwhile, my family relentlessly
pressured me to marry a suitor
they would find and bring to me
each passing day."

"So what! Learn to face life."

"But, sir,
what if life itself
withdraws from the battle?
Then what, sir?"

जो जीवन ही
परे हट जाए

एक सभा में मुलाकात के बाद
चैट पर बताती है एक लड़की
कि आत्महत्या करनेवाले
बहुत खींचते हैं उसे
यह क्या बात हुई ...
यूँ मेरे प्रिय लोगों की लिस्ट में भी
आत्महंता हैं कई
वान गॉग, मरीना, मायकोवस्की
और मायकोवस्की की आत्महत्या के पहले
आधीरात को लिखी कविता तो खींचती है
तारों भरी रात की मानिंद

पर आत्महनन मेरे वश का नहीं
सोचकर ही घबराता हूँ कि
रेल की पटरी पर मेरा कटा सर पड़ा होगा
और पास ही होगा नुचा चुंथा धड़

पर मेरे एक मित्र ने भी
हाल ही कर ली आत्महत्या
नींद की गोलियां खाकर

ठीक ही तो था
मेरी ही तरह हँसमुख

हाहाहा
क्या मैं अब भी हँसमुख हूँ

नींद की गोलियां तो मैंने भी खाई थीं
पता नहीं बच गई कैसे
क्या ... पागल हो क्या ...

बहुत परेशान थी सर
प्यार किया था फिर पता चला
उसके विवाह के अलावे संबंध हैं कई
उधर घरवाले
रोज एक लड़का ढूंढ ला रहे थे

तो ... क्या हुआ
जीवन का मुकाबला करना सीखो

पर मुकाबले से जीवन ही परे हट जाये तो ...
तो सर।

Newborn leaf

A newborn leaf follows its course
through the season's path.

Two cold drops alight
and perch quietly on its tip,
as the sun peeks
through the sky,
its rays rushing to grace the leaf's face.

In pure delight,
it quivers.

एक नया पत्ता वह

मौसम की पगडंडी पर
चल निकला
एक नया पत्ता वह

शीत के कण दो
आ ठहरे कोरों पर

बे- आहट
फलक पर
उझक रहा सूर्य

भागी भागी आ रहीं
किरणें
धुला रहीं मुख उसका

हर्ष से
कच - कचा रहा वह।

Countries that fly

There existed a country called Afghanistan
that boarded an airplane and flew
to Tashkent and America,
and a new country emerged— Islamic Emirate,
entering the same land
riding guns, bullets, and missiles.

This is the advent of the new digital world.

हवाई यात्रा करते देश

एक देश था अफगानिस्तान
हवाई जहाज पर बैठ चला गया जो
ताशकंद - अमेरिका
बंदूक की गोलियों और मिसाइलों पर सवार
एक नया देश इस्लामिक एमिरेट...
दाखिल हो गया उसी सरजमीं पर ...

नया डिजिटल विश्व है यह।

Lonely as the stars are

I experience loneliness,
much like the stars do,
those stars
that shimmer in isolation
and ultimately diminish.

They are as solitary
as a civilization
that has achieved its zenith.

They are as alone
as a child reaching for a lit candle
in a bustling household.

जैसे अकेले हैं तारे

अकेला हूँ मैं
जैसे
अकेले हैं तारे
सारे के सारे
टिमटिमाते हैं अकेले
और टूट जाते हैं ...

अकेले हैं वे
शिखरों को छूती सभ्यता
अकेली है जैसे

अकेला है वह
भरे हुए घर में
मोमबत्ती की लौ की ओर
बढ़ता बच्चा

अकेला है जैसे ...।

I am a Hindu

Because I am a Hindu, they are Muslim and Christian.
Because I am a skinner, they are Brahmin and Dushadh.

Our existence today is not a reflection
of the country's diversity;
we are so similar that only our mutual hatred
gives us a sense of identity.

In general, we are commoners:
constables, priests, maulvis, scholars, sweepers, tanners,
potters, Lalbegis, and many other things—
because we are not
doctors, engineers, politicians,
lawyers, collectors, contractors, or commissioners.

While they have access to clubs,
five-star hotels, and Air India services,
We have mandirs, masjids, churches,
parks, and grounds,
marked by violence and intractable conflicts
all in the name of political fanaticism.

We are reserved,
and that's why we get reservations

in temples, mosques, and workplaces—
where we are admitted
not based on our merit and devotion
but our incompetence, which renders us
as pawns of emperors and their slaves.

मैं हिन्दू हूँ

मैं
हिन्दू हूँ
इसलिए
वे
मुसलमान और ईसाई हैं
जैसे
मैं चर्मकार हूँ
इसलिए वे
बिरहमन या दुसाध हैं

आज हमारा होना
देश-दिशा के अलगावों का सूचक नहीं
हम इतने एक से हैं
कि आपसी घृणा ही
हमारी पहचान बना पाती है
मोटा-मोटी हम
जनता या प्रजा हैं
हम
सिपाही पुजारी मौलवी ग्रंथी भंगी
चर्मकार कुम्हार ललबेगिया और बहुत कुछ हैं
क्योंकि हम
डॉक्टर इंजीनियर नेता वकील कलक्टर
ठेकेदार कमिश्नर कुछ भी नहीं हैं

उनके लिए क्लब हैं
पांच सितारा होटल हैं
एअर इंडिया की सेवाएं हैं

हमारे लिए
मंदिर - मस्जिद - गिरजा
पार्क और मैदान हैं
मार नेताओं के नाम पर
और उनमें ना अंट पाने के झगड़े हैं

हम आरक्षित हैं
इसलिए हमें आरक्षण मिलता है
मंदिरों - मस्जिदों - नौकरियों में
जहाँ हम भक्ति और योग्यता के आधार पर नहीं
अक्षमताओं के आधार पर
प्रवेश पाते हैं
और
बादशाहों और गुलामों के
प्यादे बन जाते हैं।

Beyond Nationalist Ideals

The country wishes to honor me,
yet it remains unaware
that I have not had a proper meal in days.
At this moment, all I crave is food.

The country wants to broaden
the roads for me,
without realizing that wider roads
will only exacerbate my suffering
in every direction.

The country aspires to elevate me
as a symbol of patriotism,
but will it ever grasp
that my loyalty doesn't stem
from nationalist ideals,
but rather from the principles
of *Vasudhaiva Kutumbakam,*
embedded in Indian culture?

The nation yearns to embrace me
with its expansive chest,
but when will the nation comprehend

that I too bear a chest
with a beating heart,
though not as broad as
that of a bull or a lion,
but one that is human—
gentle and kind.

देशभक्ति मूल
का नहीं

देश मेरा सम्मान करना चाहता है

पर देश को पता नहीं कि मैं भूखा हूँ

फिलहाल मुझे रोटी की जरूरत है

देश मेरे लिए सड़कें चौड़ी करना चाहता है

क्या देश को पता है कि चौड़ी सड़कों से मेरी विपदा

और भासेगी दसो दिशाओं में

देश मुझे देशभक्त के सबूत के तौर पर

पेश करना चाहता है

पर क्या देश को कभी यह समझ आएगी कि

मैं देशभक्ति मूल का नहीं

भारतीय संस्कृति के वसुधैवकुटंबकम मूल का हूँ

देश मुझे अपने चौड़े सीने में समेटना चाहता है

पर देश को कब पता चलेगा कि मेरे पास भी

धड़कते दिलवाला एक सीना है

भले वह बैल या शेर सा चौड़ा-चकला नहीं हो

पर वह मनुष्यों सा है

नाजुक - रहमदिल।

People are good

People are good,
and bad too.
People are necks,
and knives too.
It is well within their control
to be unbending,
but people turn acquiescent
when they are helpless.
In despair,
people break
yet remain human.
In the smallest of joys,
they burst into tears,
In the smallest of sorrows,
their hearts sink.

भला होता है आदमी

भला होता है आदमी
बुरा होता है
गला होता है आदमी
छुरा होता है
आदमी के वश में होता है
सीधा होना
बेबस होता है
तो वह मुड़ा होता है

मुसीबतों में
टूट भी जाता है आदमी
टूट कर भी
आदमीयत से जुड़ा होता है

छोटी सी ख़ुशी में
फूट पड़ता है आदमी
छोटे से गम में
वह नेमुरा होता है।

Inside the shoes

When I slide my feet into my shoes,
it feels like I'm burying my head inside.
Soon, I hear the familiar sound,
'Pat Pat'
The shoes can't tolerate
any noise louder than their own
and seem eager to kick it away.
In doing so, they rise
above my own head.

जूते में

जूते में अपना पाँव डालते ही
लगता है
कि सिर डाल रहा होऊँ
फिर वही एक आवाज़ गूँजने लगती है
ठक-ठक
ठक-ठक से ऊँचा कोई भी स्वर
हो जाता है असह्य
जिसे उड़ा देना चाहता है जूता
अपनी ठोकरों में
और ऐसा करते
अक्सर वह
मेरे अपने ही सर से
ऊपर उठ जाता है।

Besieged Warrior

I'm a vulnerable human being.
It's not my bravery or my resolve
that decides if I'm a patriot or an outsider,
if I'm a betrayer or a martyr;
instead, it's a dividing line
that sets my identity.
A boundary
on either side of which
the songs of arms trafficking play incessantly,
and I've come to understand
that lauding these composers of turmoil
ensures lasting security for a nation.

घिरा हुआ योद्धा

मैं एक लाचार मनुष्य
मेरा साहस और जीवट नहीं
बल्कि एक सीमारेखा
परिभाषित करती है मुझे
कि मैं देशभक्त हूँ या घुसपैठिया
गद्दार हूँ या शहीद।
एक सीमारेखा
जिसके दोनों ओर
हथियारों की दलाली के नगमे
बजते रहते हैं अविराम
और इन नगमाकारों को
सलामी बजाते रहने से
सुनते हैं के एक राष्ट्र
सुरक्षित रहता है
अनंतकाल तक।

नोट्स

नोट्स